Reeya Jafar

The author of the book of poems titled "The Age of Wonders" is Reeya Jafar, an 11-year-old girl living in Kuwait, originally from Kannur, Kerala, India. Reeya has a deep love for reading, traveling, and writing, which she began at the age of five. So far, she has read over 900 books. Reeya is a presenter on Kuwait National TV, where she introduces various types of books to young children. Her imaginative mind and curiosity are evident in her childhood dreams, such as wanting to collect a piece of a cloud. She has many dreams about what she wants to be when she grows up, and these dreams change often as she becomes fascinated by new things she sees or experiences. Her book "The Age of Wonders" beautifully captures the innocence and awe that define childhood.

English Language
The Age of Wonders
(Poems)
by
Reeya Jafar

◆

Published in September 2024
by Kairali Books Private Limited
Thalikkavu Road, Kannur.
Ph : 0497-2761200
E-Mail : kairalibooksknr@gmail.com

◆

Cover Design
Aromal O. P.

◆

51/24-25/Sl.No.1618/200/NS.18.6
ISBN 978-93-5973-091-2

The Age of Wonders

Reeya Jafar

Kairali Books

Reeya's poems, while still having the tenderness of a child's gentle touch, do not shy away from addressing some of the grave issues faced by mankind today like the destruction of nature, discrimination based on colour, and various forms of violence. Her lines are simple, communicative, and rhythmic. I wish her a bright future as a poet.

K. Satchidanandan

DEDICATION

To my family

ACKNOWLEDGEMENT

The author expresses her heartfelt thanks to the renowned poet K. Satchidanandan, who patiently reviewed her poems and suggested many corrections. His gracious agreement to write a few lines about her poems, which are included in this book, felt like receiving an award.

A special thank you goes to Meenakshi Sharma, Assistant Editor at the Times of India, for writing a wonderful preface that perfectly captures the heart of this collection. Her kind and thoughtful words have greatly enriched the book, giving readers a meaningful introduction to the themes and feelings expressed in these poems.

The author extends sincere gratitude to the publisher, whose backing has been instrumental in bringing this book to life in its current form.

Finally, the author expresses her deepest appreciation to her parents and her sister, Reema Jafar, for their invaluable support and encouragement, which played a crucial role in the completion of this book.

Preface

A thought provoking collection of forty eight poems from an energetic young writer Reeya Jafar, strikes deep into the hearts transporting us back to the cherished memories and innocence of childhood. The anthology which is now offered to public speaks about the importance of beautiful childhood days to be treasured to many evils prevalent in society discriminating people on the basis of colour, agony of war and cruelty of the world.

Through her rhythmic lines, she reminds us of the importance of treasuring the simple joys and beauty that can be found even amid darkness. The poems underscore how freedom is not just a privilege but a fundamental human right that should be accessible to all. In our often self-absorbed modern age, Reeya's work is a powerful reminder to never forget our roots and to uphold the virtues of compassion and justice.

With an energetic yet refined style, this collection has the ability to resonate deeply across diverse audiences. Whether read in solitude or shared aloud, these poems have the power to stir the soul while imparting profound truths about the human experience. Reeya's debut is a triumph - a resonant and impactful artistic statement from a brilliant young voice.

"Lest the childhood days should pass, Make use of them fast. These lovely days, Shall never be eternal. Something as beautiful as childhood, There never was....."

Meenakshi Sharma
Assistant Editor, Times of India

CONTENTS

Mystery

A beautiful place yet to be uncovered
Just as every place had
With ups and downs,
Beauties and flaws,
And secrets yet to be discovered.
It wasn't all decorated and flowered
And folks were yet astonished
At what wasn't expected
Yet was seen on the outside.
Showing that not all
That glitters is precious.
Yet what seemed a little less
Left every person speechless.

•

The Age of Wonders

Lest the childhood days should pass,
Make use of them fast.
These lovely days
 Shall never be eternal.

Something as beautiful as childhood,
There never was.
No, not the best in the whole world
Can outdo childhood,
For, these precious days
Do more for you
Than anything else ever could.

•

From Darkness to Light

With head in hands,
She looked over the lands.
She was in great despair,
Something nearly nothing
Could repair.
The lands once lush and yielding
Were now barren and empty.
Searching for a solution,
She put the mind into motion.
T'was at this very hour
That her thoughts
Went from darkness to light.
Raced she to the hut,
It was quite simple,
Yet was the place,
The place that held the answer
To all problems,
And led the mind
From darkness to light.

•

The Might of a Pen

A pen is mightier than a sword,
So says the lord.
A pen can convey endless emotions;
A sword can convey only one of them all-
The one of hatred
To one and all.

To use a pen is better
Than to use a sword, for,
To hold a pen is better,
Lest one should choose
To wield a weapon,
Keep your virtues in mind
And spread peace
As far as one can find.

•

A Sought After Right

Freedom is the best of all,
Freedom is the biggest joy to the soul;
How would one feel if they had
All the luxuries in the world,
And yet, had no freedom?

That, alas is the sorrow
Caged beings must endure;
For them it is no child's play,
For, do what they may,
They can't get their freedom.

On making a chaos, which they do seldom,
It is deemed to be done out of boredom.
But no,
'Tis the cry for freedom,
A luxury which
They never can obtain.

•

A Wish Ungranted

Walking under her umbrella,
She looked anxiously about;
She wasn't smiling,
But the rain wasn't enough
To cover her pout.

It wouldn't have mattered all that much
If she could see a welcome little hutch.
Yet it wasn't to be,
For she wasn't in
A friendly little village,
But in a lonely moorland
Stretching for miles and miles ahead.

She would be glad
Had someone found her,
For she wasn't clad
In the best of clothes.
She'd give anything for a mac,
For she knew
That was what she lacked.
Wishes mayn't come true,
It all depends on what we do.

•

Discrimination

Black is beautiful,
It isn't that awful,
The color doesn't matter,
'Tis the character that does.

Come what may,
Black and white
Are as like,
As dawn and day.

Force away the discrimination,
It needs purification;
Rise up against those who discriminate,
For, it's never too late.

•

Dawn

At dawn, what's better to do
Than relax on a shady lawn,
Watching the bright stars fade away.
When the sun rises,
The colors of dawn make their way
Through the early morning sky,
Lighting it up
Like a raging forest fire.
Soon, the world's awake,
And so is the sun's reflection
Shining down at the lake.

•

A Precious Treasure

There once was a stone wall
That stood behind the great hall,
 And children used it
As the playground for all.

Yet, folks decided its downfall,
Leaving the children
With nothing at all.
The kids formed a clan,
And an even better plan.

They brought its good parts
Into the picture,
'Cause it kept out burglars
And kept in treasures.

At long last, it was consented,
Leaving them glowing
With growing pleasure.

Children rejoiced,
Leaving the others with no choice,
But to join in
For the stopping of the downfall
Of the great stone wall.

•

The World

The world has joys and troubles,
Surprises and tumbles.
Learn to cope,
Rather than to sit by and mope.
Everything has a way out,
And to still stay stout.
When in doubt,
Choose the right path,
Join the pieces of the puzzle,
And do the math.

•

Broken Wings

It was a moment of great despair,
Seemingly nothing could be repaired.
To try she'd dared,
But not better had she fared.
Yet bore a steady head
Through the hardships,
By which she was led.
These are the bird's legs
Through its time of broken wings.
Yet life helps us to swing,
Through times of such, with willpower
And bloom like a flower.
Let not broken wings weigh you down,
For life has more to offer
Than frets and frowns.
Always see the best in life,
Live without acts
That cut through life
As sharp as a knife.

•

A Helping Hand

Shivering with cold,
To ask for help,
She was not so bold.
To the blizzard she had lost,
The life she'd known;
But life had shown
That she mustn't moan.
There were many,
Much more unfortunate than she,
And even more,
Who turned a deaf ear to their plea.
Life can change in moments,
From royal to peasant;
Few are the people who count their blessings,
And at any moment
Life can change its setting.

•

The World Must Move On

Whether the sun has set
Or the moon has risen,
The world must move on.

Whether one has gone
Or another has come,
The world must move on.

We must accept
The happenings of the world,
And never let them weigh us down;
And in your mind,
Never put up a frown.

●

The Impossible

They said it couldn't be done,
But could it?
They said the world was a cube,
But was it?
It could be done,
The journey of discovery
Had only just begun.
There was plenty
Yet to be found;
And when uncovered,
The whole world would it astound.

•

The Right Choice

The whistling wind brushing her head,
Thought she about what was said;
It wasn't her only choice,
But was the one
For which she was poised.

There were countless roads to go down,
But she deemed none
To be finer than this one.
There wasn't another chance
To undo the wrong,
Yet there were chances
To make this world a better place,
To right what had been a mistake.

●

A Wonderous World

A beautiful place filled with wonders,
Where every petal, every leaf was valued,
And not even a single grain of sand left out,
Where people respected the wonders of the world,
And let not a resource go waste.

A place where none would go unfed,
And upon even grass
Lightly did folks tread;
Where everyone was united
And none divided;
Where people lived a simple life
And lived on without strife;
And were quite tethered
To one another.
In a place of togetherness,
Life is deemed perfect.
Reigned by peace,
One of the greatest of leaders.

•

A Mark to be Made

It was a mark to be made,
A foot print that'll always stay.
It was a daring mission,
An ambition to be fulfilled.

All were thrilled,
It was their moment
To prove themselves
As worthy of this,
An opportunity they couldn't miss.

A mark that couldn't be wiped
By the winds of the time,
It was an imprint
Not just on the moon,
But in everyone's heart.

It couldn't be forgotten,
For it was well earned and gotten.
It is still remembered
And many has it inspired;
A mark made for ever.

•

The Path of Kindness

Steer clear of cruelty
And look upon hurt creatures with pity.
They are one of us,
And we must be careful
Of what one does.
All under the sky
Are to be deemed the same;
For those who do not,
There shall only be shame.
For good creatures,
There shall only be happiness
As is known without a guess,
Evil shall receive its due,
And are forever enveloped
By a dark hue.

•

The Colors of Bliss

Spreading the joy of their colors wide,
As far as one could find.
Everything of the kind
Could dazzle the mind,
Let not little troubles
Harness you into despair,
For they can bind you, unaware.
There's always joy to be found
From the sky, to the ground.

Always believe, from the heart's center,
That there is happiness
Yet to enter.
Do not forget, with time,
That joy does not cost
Even a dime;
But is worth more
Than all the gold
In the Earth's core.

•

Blessings

A blessing isn't something special
That none in the world have;
They're the simple treasures in life
That bring no strife.

The truly priceless things
In the world
Aren't striking at first sight,
Yet aren't to be taken light.

Upon these treasures does life lean,
And to protect them must we be keen;
At all times remember,
That they are needed forever.

•

Dreams

Should dreams go unfulfilled,
There are others
At which ye are better accomplished.

Build your own life,
Only then, shall it not be cluttered with strife.
Let life take you elsewhere,
With fortune made
Fair and square.
Do your part in the world,
See true beauty unfurled.

•

The Roots of Habits

Old habits die hard,
Uproot them before they go afar.
It isn't a matter of just a day,
But, of your future.

Beware of how you handle them,
If taken care of well,
It can make you the perfect gem.
Make your presence awaited,
And wholly undebated.
Be the ray of light
In a thunderstorm;
Bring a surprise,
In a huge transform.

•

Peace of the Soul

The empathy of her heart
Was on the rise,
And with it
Did her soul shine.

All in the world have empathy in 'em,
Making them shine
As bright as a gem.

Helping you through your hardships
Will be your kind words,
Echoing from others lips.

You get back
What you give others;
And being kind at heart
Will render the soul,
As light as a feather.

There are diverse ways to be at mind,
The choice is yours of what kind;
Uphold the virtues
And like a flower shall you blossom,
And your soul shall stay forever handsome.

•

Peace At Mind

In peace at mind,
Her thoughts wandering
Where no one could find.
The troubles of the world
Leaving for once,
The blessings coming back in heaps.

She was in a place where no one had ever been,
Where there was neither crime nor sin.
A land where birds always flew
And people could touch the clouds.

A land where people
Were at perfect peace,
Which could never cease;
This could be really done,
Although it might seem tough.

•

Majestic Nature

The divine beauty of the hillsides breathtaking,
Standing in place as would a king.
Majestic yet humble,
So sturdy it would not crumble.

Should the mighty mound fall,
There would be great destruction to all.
Nature has its reasons
For even the seasons.

All in the world may
Or may not have their own way.
Every creature deserves to live,
For, big or small,
They all have something to give.

•

The Power of Knowledge

Knowledge is power,
Not taking us anywhere lower.
'Tis for our upkeep
To the top with a giant leap.

Work hard you should,
'Cause it's for your own good.
Follow your heart's desire
And life could not get finer.

Acquire knowledge for its glory,
And make a mark in history.
Be wise about the choices,
And for all consequences
You must be poised.

•

A Binding Power

The ambience of the festival blinding,
The unity in the air binding,
Sounds of laughter in the atmosphere,
Without sadness or a tear.

Recalling happy times together,
Making time go by in a blur.
United we must stand,
In each and every land.

Divided we fall,
Without any chance at all.
Listen to your heart,
And change the world as quick as a dart.

•

The Ocean of Life

Life has its ups and downs,
The difference is,
Who reaches the shore
 and who drowns.

Plant in your heart
The strongest of willpower,
And above you, opportunities shall tower.
Use every resource at hand,
For there is no saying,
Where we might land.

Hold yourself together at all times,
For everything is precious,
Even the smallest dime.

•

A Choice That Matters

The day shall end,
Whether or not there are wrongs to amend.
Cherish every moment,
Show what you really meant.

Express your deepest insights,
Leaving the rest to say as they might.
At the end of the day,
It is your choice.

Stay firm, and don't let your thoughts sway,
Be courageous and stay strong,
For to your destiny,
It couldn't be all that long.

•

Spirit

The gloom seeming to swallow her spirit,
And set before her the limit,
Yet she made it through,
Doing what she could do.

Let not hurtful words penetrate,
For they are soaked up
At an alarming rate.
Be it your fate or not,
Give it all you have got.

•

The Sea Forever

As gray, as you would never like to touch;
As gray, as you would never like to behold;
As gray, as you would never like to draw near;
As gray, as you would never like to create.

Nature is needed by all,
Nature needs all;
Water is needed by all,
Water needs all.

It shall be as blue, as you would love to touch;
As blue, as you would love to behold;
As blue, as you would love to draw near;
As blue, as you would love to
And must create.

•

Follow Your Heart

Get not swayed by the thoughts of others,
For in time,
Your own will wither.
Follow your heart,
All the way from the start.
Do what seems to be best,
Even in the toughest of tests.
A huge difference will it make,
And hardly anything will it take.

●

Feelings

Let out your breath,
Take in a rainbow,
It shows that
Not all feelings are shallow,
And watch the beauty
After a thunder storm.

Let not its dark clouds
Surround the mind,
For then we'll find ourselves in a bind;
Keep a clear head,
And never see red.

Don't unleash anger,
For then, we forget
Where to drop anchor.
Keep yourself in control,
And spread happiness in your soul.

•

Diversity

People of many a kind,
Come together in a bind,
Leaving bad times and misery behind.

In all this world,
Not everything can unfold.
That's how it works,
Even where evil lurks.
Be the person you wish to be,
Even if others disagree.

•

The Maze of Life

Looking around the maze,
He walked around in a daze,
Yet was not ready to laze.
Had I not entered this place,
Thought he,
This isn't where I would be.
One has to be wise,
Even at the smallest sacrifice.
Life has its ins and outs,
Fulfill 'em before it all mounts.
Many a time has man regretted his actions,
Even as they ended up to his satisfaction.

•

The Ticking Clock of Time

All must be on time,
Be it the sunrise,
Or just being nice,
It shall bring no strife.

Being on time,
Shall shine on you the light;
The light leading down the path of humanity and
kindness,
Which turns life into blissful foreverness.

•

The Courage of the Heart

Peering down the flight,
She looked at the fearful height;
Should I back off?, thought she
And just let my dreams be,
This was a once-in-a-life-chance,
 She thought, with another glance.

The countdown whistled in her ear,
Nothing was there to fear;
She jumped and her blood thumped,
Feet touching the ground;
She was more elated than she might sound,
There has to be in the heart some courage,
For it gives you the right message.

•

The Moon

The Sun has set,
And the moon has risen,
It's a sure bet.
The sun has sailed across the sky,
And the moon has come to take its place, up high.
The moon shedding light for the world,
Most of 'em all cozy and curled.

The night is peaceful,
With the pale moon shining,
Looking just plain beautiful.
Until the colors of dawn
Shoot across the sky,
And there, shall they lie.

•

Lies

Once you begin to tell lies,
It can never be improvised;
The truth must reign,
For it saves others from pain.

You will never be believed after a lie,
Because, there will be many ends to tie;
Better not do so,
Else, you can't keep up with the flow.

On the worse end,
Things will be harder to amend;
Stick to the better side,
Its simpler to abide.

●

The Race of Determination

Perspiration on his forehead,
And determination as tough as lead,
Off his feet pounded,
As the beginning signal sounded.

Off they raced
On the route traced,
Then he stumbled
And to the ground he crumpled;
Yet, not losing hope,
And not sitting around to mope,
Up and away was he,
As sure as can be.

In matter of moments,
Before anyone could comment,
He had come in first;
It's a lesson to learn,
With sheer determination,
You can win everyone's admiration.

•

The Pair of Nature

The lush green ground,
The clear blue that seemed sky bound,
Breathing the fresh cool air,
She deemed them to be quite a perfect pair.

Relaxed, watching the calm ripples in the water,
Pondering on how nature was fond of all living
beings;
May be not in a clear manner,
Although it couldn't be kinder.

•

War

The air thick with smoke,
Harming much more than a few folk,
It was the beginning of the end,
Which left many with themselves for to fend.

 A blast shook the ground,
The cries of people drowned,
By huge crashes of skyscrapers,
Ripped from the base.

The very essence of the place lost,
With a huge cost,
It caused no glee,
Only causing people to flee.

A boom in the sky,
Causing millions to die,
There were, in this war,
No winners, only losers.

●

The Ocean's Way

Where the ship once lay
In the bay,
There was nothing to fill in her place,
For she had left on her maiden voyage.

T'was a great night to begin with,
All at once, the wind began to blow
And the water to flow;
Cries all around,
And just as had begun,
The wind ceased to blow
And the water to flow;
It was the magic of the sea, said they,
And we shall let it be.

They sailed over the seas
And under the stars,
Who watch them from the sky
And let them safely pass.

•

Love

Love is the greatest adventure,
Into which ever a man can venture.
Love is the seed of relation,
And then a young sapling will it be,
And then into a big old tree.
Old does it become, firm will it stay,
So firm it will never sway.

•

The Music of Hope

The music washing over her,
In a low yet beautiful murmur;
Swaying her mind,
Helping her out of the bind.

The gentle whispers of hope
Helped her find a scope;
She let it lead her
To the answer.

She had believed,
And her trust in life
Had been retrieved.
The magic of a small act,
Had changed what might have been
A terrible, yet true fact.

•

The Glowing Light

The glowing fire
Looking astonishingly bright,
And even readier to fight.
She needed it to work,
Even more so in this murk.

Glowing in the darkest of nights,
Ever present to provide light;
Its embers, never ready to go,
And its flames
Dancing in a forever graceful flow.

In a world that gets so dark,
It is fire
That really makes a mark;
It never will pose a threat,
What it really means,
We mayn't know yet.

•

The Patrons of Knowledge

The wheels in her mind turning,
As she closed the last page,
She knew it would help her,
No matter what the age.

It is an endless treasure,
That could help her to no measure.
They were what she needed now,
And to them, she would bow.

Books are the treasures of this world,
And help us behold the world's true beauty unfurled.
They mayn't seem beautiful
Although it's invaluable,
And their power is unbelievable.

•

Nature's Worth

She felt the soft white under her toe,
It was clear, that it was snow.
The time of fun had arrived,
And with it, of leaves trees were deprived.

The shouts of joy in the cool breeze,
Watching the cold pond freeze.
People skating on the frozen water,
And the unmistakable sound of laughter.

She looked around with new eyes,
Thinking that it was indeed paradise.
Whether below or above the earth,
Its time we saw its worth.

Small yet important,
Yet that it wasn't useful,
Some stayed adamant.
All is of great value,
Even the smallest drop of dew.

•